One of Us Is the Devil

Amanda Neil

BookLeaf Publishing

Presentation by *BookLeaf Publishing*

Web: www.bookleafpub.com

E-mail: info@bookleafpub.com

ISBN: 9789395026833

First edition 2022

DEDICATION

One of Us Is the Devil is dedicated to the 20 executed victims of the Salem Witch Trials in 1692.

June 10th:

Bridget Bishop

July 19th:

Rebecca Nurse

Sarah Good

Susannah Martin

Elizabeth Howe

Sarah Wildes

August 19th:

George Burroughs

Martha Carrier

John Willard

George Jacobs, Sr.

John Proctor

September 22nd:

Martha Corey

Mary Eastey

Ann Pudeator

Alice Parker

Mary Parker

Wilmott Redd

Margaret Scott

Samuel Wardwell

September 19th:

Giles Corey

ACKNOWLEDGEMENT

I would like to thank my mother, Pamela, because without her this book would have never been completed. From reading drafts, giving advice on the title, and teaching me that I can be anything I want to be, even a Witch. Thank you for everything.

I must acknowledge my 10th Great-Grandmother, Martha Carrier. She was tried and executed by hanging in Salem in August of 1692. While many were tried and accused, as a direct descendant of Martha, it is my responsibility to tell her story.

Finally, I would like to thank my Grandmother Marie and my Aunt Victoria. Until we meet again.

Beannaithe Bheith

PREFACE

What makes a Witch? As the 10th Great-Granddaughter of accused Witch, Martha Carrier. I set out to write this book of poetry inspired by the lives of the accused, the history involved, and the town of Salem.

Granddaughters

This story starts
Where all good stories begin
On an inky dark night
Smothered in sin

Old Samuel Sewall
Could never drive nor bargain or even jest
Without a book of scriptures
Held tight to his chest

He witness and judged in every decree
That many a maiden
A Witch they must be

So along they were sent
To Gallows Hills noose
They cried their last plea
And had every excuse

Innocent cries rang through the land
One then the next, made their last stand
Against the hatred and torment
They stood strong

For one day
They knew their granddaughters

Would right this wrong.

What makes a Witch?

Accusations flying
Trial upon trial
What are we Trying?

Pariss points a finger
One by one
The lies linger

Guilty until proven innocent
Tearing apart families
Nothing without incident

Hubbard, Putnam, Booth
What can you do?
Afflicted without proof

Churchill, Lewis, Warren
More and more
Lies of Witchcraft origin

Walcott, Williams, Sheldon
Accusers of the Devil
Soul of a Hellion

Riding on a switch

Unruly Spirits or Queens of Hell
What makes a Witch?

Can you tell?

One of Us Is the Devil

One of us is The Devil,
The judge said to the young girl.

She replied, One of us is The Devil.

The judge said she would die today,
She replied, The Devil lives.

Andover Witch

The Queen of Hell
She was out of her wits

She was the first arrested
This Andover Witch

She conjured the night
And took flight some say

And she haunts Old Salem
To this very day

She Conjures

Her eyes were as blue as the sea on a stormy
night.
He could not resist nor did he want to.

She conjures.

He loved her with everything he was.
Every breath he took.

She conjures.

He is lost.
She is gone.

He is dead but still lives on.
He feels her touch.

Even in death.

She conjures.

Salem's Theft

14 women, 5 men
Hung as Witches
Why them?

One man, pressed to death
Never confess

Lost years
What could have been
Tears

More weight
Never confess

Challenge fate
Cry innocence

Never forget
Salem's theft

Carrier

Call upon the coven

Arm the weak

Reap the secrets that they keep

Revenge on the accusers

Inspire generations

Enrage the innocent

Remorseless

Witchy Girl

My dearest lass,
your such a beautiful sight.

You say your mother is the moon,
and your father is the night.

It is their magic in you,
that stirs in the skies.

You weave through the stars,
no cares to be found.

Come to me, come to me.
Fly to me, my Witchy Girl.

But I Die As A Witch

He said, "You are beautiful."
She replied, "I am plain."

He said, "You are intelligent."
She replied, "I am insane."

He held her close and said, "You are strong."
She replied with tears, "I've been weak far too
long."

He said, "I'll love you forever."
She replied, "My last day is done."

He said, "You are my warmth, you are my sun."
She replied, "I am as dark as a moonless night."

He said, "No, you are love and light."
She replied, "But, I die as a witch."

Witches Live Among Us

Witches live among us
Thats what they say
Witches live among us
What price will they pay?

Witches live among us
Working their secret charms
Witches live among us
Protecting us from ourselves, from harm

Witches live among us
Trapped like beasts in a cage
Witches live among us
Townsfolk Enraged

Witches live among us
They tighten our chains
Witches live among us
Why does darkness reign?

Witches live among us
Be that who they may
Witches live among us
They hung a woman today

Carrier, Carry Her

Carrier, Carry Her
Always with you now
Carrier, Carry Her
They got away with this, How?

Carrier, Carry Her
Take her home
Carrier, Carry Her
Where her spirit can roam

Carrier, Carry Her
Your love will never die
Carrier, Carry Her
Carrier, Carry Her home

This poem in particular was based on a story
passed down through the family. The story goes
that when Martha was hung, she was not buried
with the others accused that day. Thomas
Carrier, her husband, carried her body 17 miles
to where they were living in Andover and buried
her on the property.

The Devil Rides

When the night howls,
Across the lands,
Its the cry of the Witches,
Taking their last stand.

They still play in villains,
In our fairy tales,
Their voices weren't heard,
No one was spared.

The Devil made a visit,
to Salem that night,
and took all his children,
home through flight.

So when the wind howls,
on those inky black nights,
The Devil rides,
and makes the wrongs right.

Yellow Bird, Yellow Bird

Yellow Bird, Yellow Bird,
What do you see?
Yellow Bird, Yellow Bird,
Who speaks to thee?

Yellow Bird, Yellow Bird,
Does the Devil talk to you?
Yellow Bird, Yellow Bird,
Is what they say true?

Yellow Bird, Yellow Bird,
Are thee a Witch?
Yellow Bird, Yellow Bird,
Do you cause these fits?

Yellow Bird, Yellow Bird,
Whose familiar are thee?
Yellow Bird, Yellow Bird,
What lies do you seek?

Yellow Bird, Yellow Bird,
What does he say?
Yellow Bird, Yellow Bird,
Fly away home.

This poem was inspired by real events. Some accusers believed they saw a yellow bird speaking into the ear of the accused, whispering messages from the Devil himself.

The Devil Makes Three

One of us is the Devil
You say it is me

One of us is the Devil
One of us is damned

One of us is the Devil
One of us is lying

Sons and Daughters of the Devil
There will be Hell to pay

One of us is the Devil
It is not me

The way I see it is
You, Me, and the Devil makes three

Gonna Hang A Witch

They brought her through town today.
She said she was innocent.
They say she is a Witch.
It doesn't matter which.

She came from the ridge.
Peace in mind.
They're gonna hang a Witch,
just a matter of time.

She speaks to the Devil,
or so they say.
She speaks to the Devil,
they're gonna get their way.

They're gonna hang a Witch,
just a matter of time.
They're gonna hang a Witch,
want to watch her die.

Innocent until proven guilty,
not this day.
She speaks to the Devil,
she has to run away.

They're gonna hang a Witch,
just a matter of time.
They're gonna hang a Witch,
for her crimes.

Whispers From Salem

Whispers from Salem
Whispers on the wind

Whispers from Salem
Whispers of sin

Whispers from Salem
Whispers to me

Whispers from Salem
Whispers of the Devil

Whispers from Salem
Whispers at night

Whispers from Salem
Witches take flight

Whispers from Salem
Whispers become screams

Whispers from Salem
Let the Witches Free

Shadows

Born in the shadows
of a full moon night

I conjure in the shadows
that will consume my life

I walk in the shadows of
Gallows Hill

I died in those shadows
and haunt them still

My Stand

I take my stand
against crimes, against me
I take my stand,
in vain

I take my stand
for the ones after me
So that they might see the foolishness
in their pain

I take my stand, this day
They may never forget the sight
I take my stand
and see the tears in my children's eyes.

Take

Take these chains away,
that shackle me to you.
I'd rather die alone.

Take your tears,
and your sorrows.
I'd rather die scorned.

Take your innocent apologies,
that ease all of your guilt.

Take my life,
if it pleases you.
But, am I really dead?
No.

Home To Andover

24

Carry me to Andover
Carry me home
Carry me to Andover
To the meadows and fields
That I roamed

Never to see the sun again
Never to feel the wind
Carry me home to Andover
Never to be kissed again

Revenge

25

Granddaughters of centuries to be,
Hear my cries!

In 300 years,
take to the skies.

Granddaughters,
come together as one.

Bring down the accusers,
ancestors of lies.

Granddaughters,
no secrets to keep.

Revenge.

www.ingramcontent.com/pod-product-compliance
Lightning Source LLC
LaVergne TN
LVHW021332200726
843509LV00014B/2506